Everyday Smiles

"A CARTOON JOURNAL"

BY DON McCLURE

JEC PUBLISHING COMPANY

2969 E. Chestnut Expy

Springfield, Missouri 65802

(800) 313-5121

www.jecpubco.com

Copyright © 2010 by Don McClure

First Edition

Library of Congress Control Number: 2010925137

ISBN: 978-0-9826424-6-7

Author & Cartoonist: Don McClure

Editing Contributions by: Pam Eddings

Prepared for Publishing by: JE Cornwell & Carolyn Cambronne

Printed in USA

Don and I had our first date on October 20, 1956 after seeing each other for the first time in the ninth grade in 1952. I had no idea that he could draw cartoons until he started doing them to entertain my little sisters and brothers.

Shortly after we were married October 19, 1957, he started his own sign business and began using his artistic ability. I was impressed most when he did a portrait of a man running for the Justice of the Peace on a billboard. I thought, "This husband of mine is good!" He began creating unusual signs, then carving and gold leafing them.

Don enjoyed leaving me notes and little cartoons to find after he left the house. I enjoyed sending him cards and sticking notes in his pockets, although I don't have any artistic ability to speak of. About ten years ago, he started leaving cartoons and little notes on the counter. He was making them on paper towels, so I encouraged him to do them on 4x6 cards. That started the every morning cartoons that I've saved, and when we were getting all the albums out, I decided to weigh them. I was surprised to learn that I had 30 pounds of his cartoons.

First thing Don did every morning was to go down the drive and get the newspaper and put it on the bed for me to have when I woke up. Then he would do the cartoon before eating or anything else. When I see the cartoon, it feels like Christmas and my birthday all rolled into one...and this happens at least once every day! The cartoons usually have something to do with something I said or did, or whatever is going on in our life. He writes a journal every day, but this has turned out to be a cartoon journal of our life. Several years ago, he came up with some characters named Bud and Bert, Beulah and Pearl, Junior, Whiskers and Mooch the dog, and Mincemeat the cat (which isn't around very often!).

One day after watching people carving things at Silver Dollar City, Don said, "I can do that!" and he bought some tools to start carving things. He had so much fun chipping away the wood to find what he already knew was hiding in there!

Some people wonder if there is anything that he can't do, and I tell them, "Yes, he can't cook!" He writes poems and songs, and the other night he woke up at 3:00 am and wrote down the words to a song as they came to him. He sang the song to me, and I played it and recorded it on tape. That night, he sang it in church. Oh, I forgot...he sings beautifully, and when we were in high school, I played the piano for the boys' Glee Club. Don sang in that group, but I didn't know how good he was then. Later I walked into a church where he was the Pastor and heard this beautiful song playing and was shocked to see him standing in the empty auditorium with a mike, singing his heart out! Wow! That is when we started doing more specials. He's played the harmonica most of his life and took up the banjo in his late thirties. He can even tune a piano...so why can't he cook? He watches all the cook shows on TV and the rest of his family loves to cook!

When we were married, I hoped that we would grow old and be best friends, and we are. I thank God for blessing us all of these years. On our 52nd wedding anniversary last year, I promised him twenty-five more!

I would like to thank everyone who has encouraged us to get his cartoons published. I hope they bless you as much as they have blessed me.

Vivian Aldrich McClure

The Main Characters

Back Row Left to Right: Bud, Whiskers and Bert.
Front Row Left to Right: Junior, Pearl, Beulah and Mooch.

In the Beginning

It was just Black and White

Then Came Color...

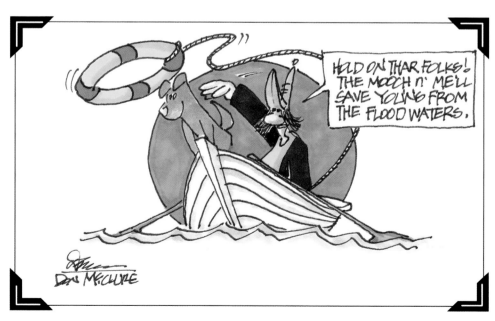

How we felt after talking to the publisher!

*I get so tired on trips that I told Don I'd love to be
pulled on Roller Skates...*

Don always agreeing with people he overhears talking!

My hands were freezing and his body was soooo warm!!!

True story of Crevan who is five years old.

True story of Elyssa and Keirsten reading the bible.
(Daddy won't eat tomatoes.)

Thanks to all the "Doctors" at the Baldknobbers
in Branson, MO

Sister fell over the cliff while helping her husband
at the lake!

Bud kissing my sister Jan good-bye!

Diane was a Gospel singer from Maine.

They were missionaries there!

Bud Everett at the wheel of his new car!

Kenny and I became friends after he changed the tire
on my car in Ash Grove.

Found out the next day that it was my brother in-law who was calling and not saying anything!!

Notice the 'DEPENDS' bib!!

When they're young it only takes a buck, teenagers take a fist full, old age takes a fanny pack of credit cards!!

Sometimes Vivian gets creative!!

Did you notice the jet engine strapped to the Yoder's horse?

A girl spider wouldn't show up around a swatter!!!

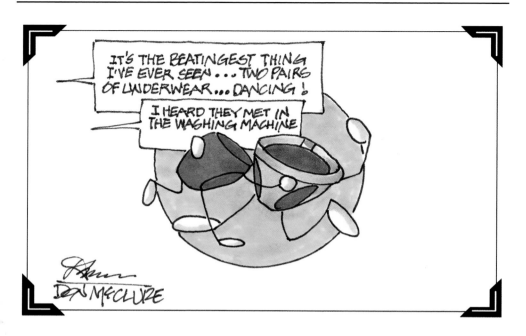

Larry O'Brian Director

American Idol has nothing on us!

Rabbits are scarce in Maine and the Governor announced he
was going to correct this!

Must be what our two stained glass parrots say!!

Ants continue to march on our porch railing in Maine!

Interpretation of a Mexican train Domino game!

Well, one was swollen!!

Painted a sea shell for Don on Valentine's Day.

A real Cow Girl!

Oh how true!!!

Threatening to let these cows out of the barn for once!!

I should never have told him I dreamed I was pole dancing!!

What I said after we finished building our new home in Maine!

Don always says I will be warmer when I'm dead, because
I'll be room temperature!!

Baseball Season

That will teach you to strike a match in the bathroom!!!

Decided to start teaching Don how to do things in the house after I'm dead and gone!!

Don't you think he looks a little too happy?

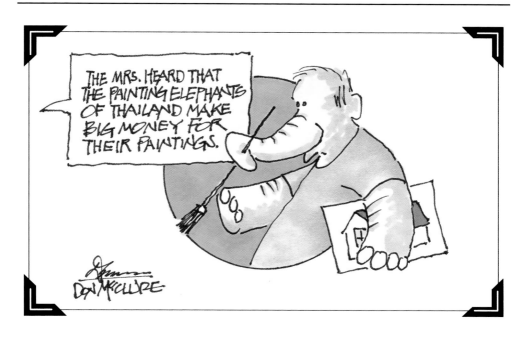

OH-OH BERT...THIS FELLA
SEEMS TO BE A LITTLE UPSET!

Y'KNOW BERT, YOU
SHUDDA BOUGHT A TRACKA!

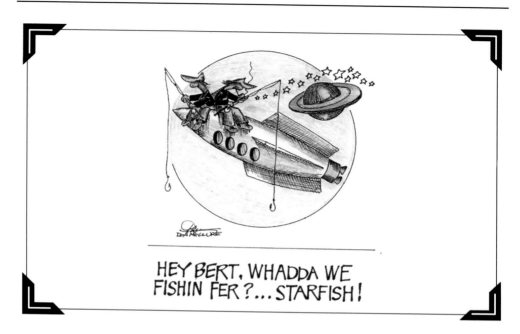

HEY BERT, WHADDA WE
FISHIN FER ?...STARFISH!

HEY BERT! THIS POOL SHOOTIN
IS FUN!...YOU MORON!
WE'RE SUPPOSED T'SHOOT POOL!

DEAR GOD, DADDY LOST HIS
JOB, WE'RE DESPERATE.
PLEASE SEND $100.00

OH GOODIE! IT'S IN THE MAIL,
SURELY GOD WILL GET IT!

SPECIAL DELIVERY FOR
LITTLE BOBBY JOE

OH GREAT! IT WENT BY WAY
OF WASHINGTON AND THEY
KEPT 95 PERCENT OF IT!

Susan Collins

November 1, 2006

Mr. Don McClure
4730 N. State Hwy. Uu
Ash Grove, MO 65604

Dear Mr. McClure,

Thank you for your kind note and the great illustration of the recent Lewiston Sun Journal article about keeping our troops warm. Your art work is amazing.

Again, thank you for your kind words. I appreciate your support.

Sincerely,

Susan

Susan M. Collins
United States Senator

SMC:rmm

What a great artist you are!

United States Senate
Washington, DC 20510

Artists Note

I always loved to draw from my earliest recollection. When I went to high school I signed up for Art class. The art teacher told me on the very first day that I'd never make it as an artist and she suggested I take a foreign language...which I did. That's where I first saw the girl that would eventually become my wife. I can say that when I saw her she had fresh daisies in her hair. I was smitten! I told my friends: "there's the girl I'm going to marry." At that time, all I had to offer was sideburns and zits. She definately was not impressed. I prevailed. We have celebrated fifty two years of marriage. My bride has encouraged my art. I keep saying it is all just "Dumb Stuff"...she says differently. What do you think?

Don McClure

Vivian Aldrich McClure